NOV 9 3

EcoZones

TEMPERATE FORESTS

Lynn M. Stone

ROURKE ENTERPRISES, INC.
Vero Beach, FL 32964

Photo Credits:

© Tom and Pat Leeson 29; all other photos © Lynn M. Stone.

© 1989 Rourke Enterprises, Inc.

Library of Congress Cataloging in Publication Data

Stone, Lynn M.
   Temperate forests / by Lynn M. Stone.
     p. cm. — (Ecozones)
   Includes index.
   Summary: Examines the forest community as an ecological niche and describes the trees, plants, and animals supported there.
   ISBN 0-86592-439-2
   1. Forest ecology—North America—Juvenile literature.   2. Forests and forestry—North America—Juvenile literature.   [1. Forest ecology.   2. Forests and forestry.   3. Ecology.]   I. Title.
II. Series: Stone, Lynn M.   Ecozones.
QH541.5.F6S76   1989
574.5'2642—dc20   89-34960
                                                  CIP
                                                      AC

CONTENTS

THE FOREST

Somehow, forests make memories. Nearly everyone in North America lives within an easy drive of a forest and has had the opportunity to be in one.

We often remember forests as cool, green retreats from the hum of cities. The quiet grandeur of forests helps millions of Americans forget their everyday existence and concerns. Especially in summer, the North American forests are a welcome break for picnickers, hikers, campers, naturalists, photographers, and artists.

But the forest isn't always calming. Memories can be of forests dark and dismal, overwhelming in their silence and isolation. Some people remember being lost among big trees, and anyone who has struggled uphill in the green dusk of a montane forest while hailstones bounced around like popcorn knows that forests are not always serene.

If some of our experiences with the great North American woodland have a dark side, it is no wonder. The forests of North America are vast, and they are tremendously varied in composition.

Opposite *Joyce Kilmer Memorial Forest is a lush, deciduous forest in North Carolina and Tennessee.*

Not all are like the "tamed" forests of suburbia or the familiar, well-traveled forests of weekenders. Even today, wild, unbroken forests, thick and tall and sprawling, still exist. These are the forests sliced by ravines of rushing water and wrenched upward by mountain crests. They are the forests where lynx, black bear, wolverine, and an occasional mountain lion are on the guest register. Enchanting, yes, but they are also demanding and unforgiving.

Because much of North America is covered with trees, we're never far from a forest. Most of Canada is forested, with the exceptions of the northern tier of tundra and the Arctic islands. Fully one-third of the lower United States is forest land as is more than half of Alaska.

The woodlands of Canada, the United States, and most of Mexico are called **temperate** forests. They occur in the Temperate Zone, the area bounded by the Arctic Circle at 66° north of the equator and the tropic of Cancer at 23½° north of the equator. Below the Temperate Zone, in southern Mexico, the Caribbean islands, and Central America are the tropical forests.

In these far-flung communities of trees, millions of animals and plants are at work. Their complex relationships to each other, and to the air, water, and soil around them, are the grist of the forest **ecosystem**. There is really nothing haphazard about the forest. As a system, its parts are in tune to each other, like the parts of a precision automobile. In some forests, you can easily see a certain orderliness. Beneath your feet lies the forest's litter layer, a carpet of leaves and twigs peppered with ferns and wild-flowers, which is the forest **herb** layer. Above the ferns and flowers is a layer of shrubs—small, woody plants—and saplings. Above the shrub layer is an

Below *The blaze of color in the broad-leaved trees of New England is one of the world's great natural spectacles.*

FORESTS

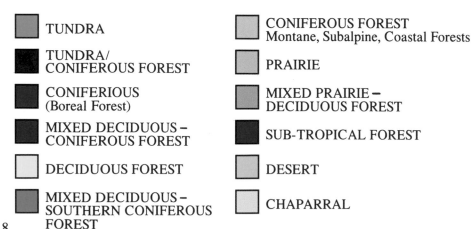

TUNDRA

TUNDRA/
CONIFEROUS FOREST

CONIFERIOUS
(Boreal Forest)

MIXED DECIDUOUS –
CONIFEROUS FOREST

DECIDUOUS FOREST

MIXED DECIDUOUS –
SOUTHERN CONIFEROUS
FOREST

CONIFEROUS FOREST
Montane, Subalpine, Coastal Forests

PRAIRIE

MIXED PRAIRIE –
DECIDUOUS FOREST

SUB-TROPICAL FOREST

DESERT

CHAPARRAL

understory of trees of moderate height and stature. Well over your head is the canopy layer of the forest, the forest's roof. It is composed of the combined crowns of the forest's tallest trees.

In general terms, North American trees are either **deciduous** or **coniferous**, broad-leaved or needle-leaved, and hardwood or softwood. The deciduous trees are true flowering plants and bear seeds within some type of closed, often fleshy capsule. Conifers produce seeds in cones. Most of the North American conifers are needle-leaved and evergreen; they do not shed their leaves each fall. Two well-known exceptions, however, are the bald cypress and the tamarack, both of which are deciduous conifers. They bear cones, but they shed their leaves.

Most of the deciduous trees are broad-leaved. Notable exceptions are the evergreen broad-leaved trees of West Indies origin that live in the southern tip of Florida.

"Hardwood" refers generally to deciduous trees rather than to conifers. The wood of such high quality, lumber-producing trees as oak and maple is literally harder when compared to many of the pines. Nevertheless, conifers furnish about 75 percent of the lumber processed in North America.

Deciduous, coniferous, and mixed forests of needle-leaved and broad-leaved trees reach around and across North America. A broad belt of conifers stretches from Alaska eastward across Canada to the Atlantic. Much of the central United States, west of the Mississippi River, is grassland. From the Rocky Mountains west to California, Oregon, and Washington, however, lie large sections of coniferous trees. East of the Mississippi nearly the entire United States was originally cloaked in trees, most of them broad-leaved. Much of the region is still forested.

Nowhere is that eastern forest more luxuriant than in the Southern Appalachian Mountains. The forest's masterpiece is Great Smoky Mountains National Park, 800 square miles of misty green slopes and valleys straddling the rugged North Carolina-Tennessee border. The park has 1,400 kinds of flowering plants, including 130 species of trees. Three hundred moss species, 230 lichens, and 2,000 fungi grow here in the largest remaining stands of virgin hardwoods in North America. Nearby in the Nantahala National Forest of North Carolina is the lush, 3,800-acre Joyce Kilmer Memorial

Forest. The forest is a living tribute to a young man who was killed in combat during the final months of World War I. Kilmer appreciated the beauty of forest trees as few others have. His poem "Trees," published in 1914, is a celebration of the forest.

The Smoky Mountains are a guaranteed good memory of the forest. So too are the autumn woodlands of Vermont and New Hampshire. The blaze of color on New England hillsides early each October is one of the world's great natural spectacles. Sugar maples draped in scarlet stand with paper birch in gold and green pines. There is a supporting cast of aspen, beech, mountain ash, wild cherry, hemlock, basswood, elm, and tamarack with their assorted hues of purple, green, red, and yellow.

In the West are the fabled aspens of Colorado autumns and the giant sequoias of the Sierra Nevada. But the towering redwood forest of California's northern coast is the western forest's crowning achievement. Nestled in moist, coastal valleys, the redwoods pitch 300 feet into their morning bath of fog. The ancient redwoods, some of them 2,000 years old, are the world's tallest living things and another unforgettable part of the North American forest.

TYPES OF FORESTS

Reduced to its simplest form, the North American forest consists of a northern belt of conifers and an eastern forest of broad-leaved, deciduous trees. Where the forests meet, a so-called mixed forest of broad-leaved and coniferous trees occurs.

If we look at the forests of North America more closely, we see major extensions of conifers into the western mountains and along the Pacific coast. A separate, predominantly conifer forest occurs in the Southeast. We also see two distinct forest types in southern Florida. One is the subtropical forest of West Indian trees. The other is the coastal mangrove forest, a wet forest of shrubby, saltwater-tolerant trees.

Based upon the dominant tree species, scientists recognize several divisions in each of the two major forest types. These divisions are created by differences in the lay of the land, soil, precipitation, and temperature.

The coniferous forest includes four major divisions: boreal, subalpine, montane, and coastal forest communities. The boreal forest is the northern forest

Opposite *Needle-leaved conifers dominate the forests of Western mountains.*

of pointed firs and spruces. It girdles virtually all of Canada south of the tundra and interior Alaska. The boreal forest spans some 4,000 miles of North America from western Alaska to Newfoundland. It dips into northern New England, New York, Michigan, Wisconsin, and Minnesota. A finger of boreal forest creeps along some of the highest elevations of the Appalachian Mountains from Maine south to Georgia.

The boreal forest is the "North Woods" of the Great Lakes states. There and elsewhere it is a region of lakes, ponds, and bogs. The northernmost bogs are called muskegs.

Below *The boreal forest spans some 4,000 miles of North America from western Alaska to Newfoundland.*

The boreal forest typically has a soft carpet of litter—twigs, cones, and needles. It is a dark place, shielded by its boughs, and the lack of sunlight discourages the growth of shrubs and smaller trees. Moss and lichens, clinging to trunks and branches, are abundant. The dominant species of trees in the boreal forest may be spruces, firs, white pines, tamaracks, or, in disturbed sites, the deciduous paper birch and aspen.

The subalpine forest is a high altitude community in the Rockies and Pacific coast ranges. Many of its trees are gnarled, twisted, and pruned by high winds. Its uppermost limits reach the treeless zone of alpine tundra, a community of grasses, lichens, mosses, and tiny flowers. Typical trees of the subalpine community are lodgepole pines and Engelmann spruce. The most unique trees in the community are the bristlecone pines living at 8,000-11,000 feet in scattered sites. Bristlecones are not big trees; their harsh environment sees to that. But they are the earth's oldest living organisms, some of them exceeding 4,000 years of age.

The montane forest of the West developed on the lower slopes of mountains, below the subalpine community. Where the grassland meets the western mountains, the montane forest soon begins.

Montane forest has richer soil and a gentler climate than subalpine. It is a denser community, too, and has larger trees. In fact, the sequoia trees of California in montane forests are the world's largest living things. The famous General Sherman tree weighs several million pounds and has bark four feet thick. The sequoias are found at altitudes between 4,000 and 8,000 feet in just 70 groves, most of them within Yosemite and Sequoia National Parks. More common members of the montane community are the ponderosa pine, sugar pine, incense cedar, and Douglas fir. The sugar pine is best known for its giant cones, some of which are 26 inches long.

The coastal forest is the most luxuriant evergreen forest in the United States or Canada. Stretching nearly 3,000 miles along the Pacific coast from a point south of San Francisco to Kodiak Island, Alaska, the coastal forest has an abundance of rain, high humidity, and moderate, sea-warmed temperatures throughout the year. Douglas fir grow here along with western hemlock and redwoods, taller and more slender trees than their close cousins, the Sequoias.

Here and there, particularly on the Olympic peninsula of Washington, are pockets of temperate rain forest, not to be confused with the tropical rain forest of Central and South America. The rain forests are lush **habitats** where precipitation can exceed 200 inches a year.

A paltry number of broad-leaved trees including aspens, alders, bigleaf maples, and certain birches, are found in the West's extensive conifer forests. But the true realm of the broad-leaved trees is the East, from northern New England and southeast Canada south to Florida and west to the prairie. Over 500

Above *The Pacific coastal rain forest of Washington State is the wettest land habitat in the continental United States.*

17

Above *Pines dominate the sandy Atlantic coastal plain.*

species of trees and shrubs grow in the eastern forests.

Several somewhat distinct divisions of the broad-leaved, deciduous forest are the northern Appalachian, southern Appalachian, central lowland, and coastal plain forests. The northern Appalachian forest covers most of New England, New York, southeast Canada, and parts of Michigan, Wisconsin, and Minnesota. In its northernmost reaches, the deciduous forest forms a border of dispute with the evergreens, primarily eastern hemlock and white pine. The northern Appalachian region is the classic

New England forest of "painted" autumn leaves.

The southern Appalachian forest of the Southeast is a highly variable forest of oaks, walnut, hickory, birches, beech, chestnut, tulip tree, sugar maple, and many others. It often has an understory of flowering dogwood and mountain thickets of various rhododendron species. One of the natural mysteries of the region is the origin of hundreds of "balds," grassy openings in the mountain forests.

The central lowland community is the westernmost portion of the deciduous forest. It reaches from the lower slopes of the Appalachian Mountains to the lowlands of the Mississippi and Ohio River valleys. Maples, oaks, hickory, beech, and streamside sycamores are among the dominants.

The coastal plain forest lies between the Appalachian Mountains and the Atlantic Ocean. This is a considerably different eastern forest community from the others, because it is dominated by the pines which thrive on the characteristic sandy soil of the region. Oaks are common here too, and the community is sometimes called the coastal pine-oak forest.

MAKING OF THE FOREST

Trees persist in cold, barren places, but even trees have their limitations. The virtually treeless tundra of the Far North and the grassland of interior North America are cases in point.

Trees have certain basic requirements. One is moisture. They need a minimum of 15 inches of rainfall each year, although some of the shrubby desert trees are an exception. They also need about three frost-free months and, of course, a place where they can put their roots down.

In the desert Southwest, most trees fail because the rainfall dwindles to fewer than 10 inches per year. In the central west, where the vegetation is prairie, or grassland, trees may have adequate moisture, but they have other problems. Prairie grasses form dense root fabrics that tend to exclude would-be invaders like trees. Additionally, prairie fires and strong, abrasive winds deter the growth of trees on the prairies.

The boreal forest fizzles in the Far North because the soil freezes permanently. Frozen soil is not a problem for a hardy tree like the black spruce if the

Opposite When farmers abandoned their New England pastures, mixed forests of conifers and broad-leaved trees reclaimed them.

soil thaws each spring to a depth of about 18 inches. But in Arctic Canada and in much of Alaska, the frozen soil, called permafrost, does not ever thaw to 18 inches. A tree cannot develop without a root structure. Although the black spruce spreads its roots horizontally, it cannot cope with so little thawed soil.

In forest development, conifers have the advantage in cold climates, where the growing season is comparatively short. One advantage is the presence of **resinous** chemicals in the needles, stems, and roots of needle-leaved trees. That chemical acts as an antifreeze so that certain conifers can weather severe winters without damage. Also, by not shedding their needles all at one time, the conifers have their leaves already in place when the ground thaws and water is available. They can immediately begin the food-manufacturing process known as **photosynthesis**.

Conifer forests are not restricted to the cold North. Several pine species are common on the southern coastal plain where fire is a normal part of the environment. Longleaf pine has **adaptations**, such as a fire-resistant bark, which allow it to survive fires that kill broad-leaved trees. Nevertheless, most of the conifer belt is in cold country where the average winter temperature may be as low as -20° F and the average summer temperature is no higher than 70°F. In warmer climates, where the growing season approaches at least 150 days annually, deciduous trees usually dominate.

For a tree to prosper, it needs sunlight, which it uses in the food-making process. The broad leaves of deciduous trees offer more exposed surface than needle leaves. In areas where the growing season is sufficiently long, the deciduous tree has the advantage in gathering the sun's energy.

Wherever they grow, trees are the dominant plants. Flowers and shrubs don't threaten trees. If left unattended, abandoned pastures and fields are taken over by trees. There is no better place to witness this example of plant **succession**, the change of plants within a community, than in the woodlands of New England.

No woodland worth its keep in New England, it seems, is without its hedges of stone wall. The stone walls were built by settlers who cut the original timber and tried desperately to farm the rocky soil. Their efforts largely failed, despite the removal of thousands of rocks which they stacked into stone walls. Today the stone walls lie hidden in the long shadows of relatively new forest, testament to the enduring qualities of the trees—and stone walls.

When the farmers abandoned their fields, dandelions, ragweed, and milkweed quickly moved in among the grasses. These early **pioneer plants** were followed by asters, goldenrod, sumac, and eventually tree pioneers, such as red cedar and aspen. As time passed, the weedy plants were crowded out by the roots and shade of the trees. The pioneer trees were probably evicted by white pines. But the white pines tended to shade out their offspring. An understory of more shade-tolerant, deciduous trees developed. The mature pines succumbed to disease and other natural causes, and the deciduous trees that grew below them ultimately dominated the forest.

Forest development is a long process, and during the time a forest struggles to reach some sort of climax stage or maturity, it undergoes constant change. The New England forest that grew up on the abandoned pasture may continue more or less in its present composition of tree species for years. On the other hand, it could be naturally altered at any time by disease, fire, or storm.

PLANTS OF THE FOREST

Next to the trees themselves, the most conspicuous plants of the forest are the wildflowers. All forests have wildflowers, but the best-known are the early spring wildflowers of the eastern forests. On the whole, the forests discourage the growth of sun-loving plants below the canopy, but in early spring,

Below *Wildflowers of the eastern deciduous forest, like the bloodroot and hepatica here, bloom before tree leaves shade the forest floor.*

sunlight dapples the forest litter and many of the wildflowers of the deciduous forest bloom before the canopy leafs out. For several weeks, from March through May, the forest floor is a wild garden of hepatica, bloodroot, trillium, violet, bellflower, anemone, and adder's-tongues. As the canopy develops and reduces the light reaching the ground, the variety and abundance of flowers slackens.

Many of the plants that like the moist, shady conditions of forest are non-flowering. These are the "primitive" non-flowering plants: fungi, lichen, moss, liverwort, hornwort, and ferns. Representatives of at least some of these plants are found in every forest. The richest, moistest forests, such as the Pacific coastal forest and the wooded valleys of the southern Appalachians, have all these interesting plants.

ANIMALS OF THE FOREST

It's relatively easy to hide in a forest, especially if you are an animal. Therefore, a silent forest actually isn't as lifeless as it may seem. Hunters of deer, squirrels, and turkeys have learned that the most effective way to find their game is to choose a likely place and wait. In other words, barging through a forest may not reveal much about the creatures that live there. Patience and practiced observation are much more useful tools to discovery in the woodlands.

You can begin discovering woodland animals by just overturning a log or stone. Underneath will be insects and other **invertebrate** animals, such as spiders, millipedes, earthworms, and centipedes. Among these little animals are plant-eaters, **herbivores**, and flesh-eaters, **carnivores**. The same categories apply to the **vertebrates**, the larger, back-boned animals. Some animals are **omnivores**, eating both plant and animal material.

In the northern coniferous forests, amphibians and reptiles are scarce. Other than the little wood frog, you are

Right *Forest sala-manders dine on the invertebrates of the forest litter, including earthworms.*

Right *Mushrooms are among the fungi, one of the forest's decomposers.*

not apt to see amphibians. The cold climate does not encourage development of vertebrates that must depend upon their environment to bring their own body temperature to a functional level, as is the case with reptiles and amphibians. Deciduous forests, on the other hand, have a fair number of amphibians and reptiles because of their longer, warmer summers and less hostile winters. They also have a variety of **aquatic** habitats that appeal especially to amphibians. Toads and salamanders live in deciduous forest along with such reptiles as box turtles, wood turtles in the Northeast, fence lizards, garter snakes, timber rattlesnakes, and copperheads.

Birds of the forests include herbivores, carnivores, and omnivores. Typical plant-eating birds of the northern forest are ruffed grouse and mountain quail. The grouse enlivens the forest each spring by making a favorite log its drumming ground. Beating its wings in a blur to attract a mate, the male ruffed grouse is the spring thunder of the forest. The goshawk, tiny boreal owl,

Below *This ruffed grouse drums on a favorite log to attract a mate in a spring ritual of northern woodlands.*

great horned owl, and great gray owl are among the northern bird carnivores.

The northern omnivores among the birds include the white-throated sparrow, chickadees, Steller's and gray jays, grosbeaks, crossbills, finches, several warblers, and both hermit and Swainson's thrushes.

In the broad-leaved forest, characteristic herbivorous birds are the wild turkey and bobwhite. Carnivores are the great horned owl, screech owl, barred owl, red-tailed hawk, red-shouldered hawk, and sharp-shinned hawk. As in the coniferous forest, most of the perching birds of the deciduous woods are omnivores. Among them are blue jays, cardinals, mockingbirds, catbirds, and several woodpecker species.

The herbivorous mammals of the northern and western conifers include several small rodents and more conspicuous rodents—red squirrels, golden-mantled ground squirrels, and marmots, the woodchucks of western mountains. Other herbivores are the varying hare, white-tail deer, elk, moose, and woodland caribou.

Characteristic carnivorous mammals of the northern evergreens are the short-tailed weasel, mink, the fox-like marten, fisher, wolverine, Canada lynx,

Opposite The red-headed woodpecker, shown at its nest hole in an oak, is one of several North American woodpecker species.

Above *Elk live in the mountain forests of the West with access to grassy meadows.*

black bear, grizzly bear, and timber wolf.

The deciduous forest, too, has a wide selection of seldom-seen, small, herbivorous rodents. Larger rodents of the woods and forest edges are the tree squirrel and the woodchuck, itself a giant ground squirrel. White-tail deer are common herbivores throughout the deciduous forest and in much of the coniferous forest as well.

The carnivorous mammals of the broad-leaved forest are the raccoon, Virginia opossum, shrew, striped skunk, bobcat, red fox, gray fox, and mink.

Many animals, particularly among the birds and mammals, have multiple forest habitats and easily adapt from one forest zone to another as it suits

their needs.

Several animals of the forest show specific **adaptations**, or strategies, for living there. Leafhoppers and katydids look very much like the leaves they settle on. Several moths, spiders, and beetles **camouflage** themselves on bark. The walking stick looks exactly like its namesake. The sharp-shinned hawk has short, round wings, for maneuverability in the woodlands. Crossbills have unique, crossed mandibles designed for easy extraction of conifer seeds. Many mammals—squirrels, raccoons, fishers, martens, opossums—are at least partly **arboreal**, capable of spending time in trees. The wood duck and several owls nest in tree holes.

Above *A white-tailed deer fawn tries to avoid detection by lying still on forest floor.*

THE FLOW OF ENERGY

The animals that live in forests do so because they find food and shelter there. The food is the source of the energy that allows them to function in their environment.

Animal food comes from plants, either directly or indirectly. Even the forest hunters depend on plants for their energy.

Sunlight is the basic source of energy on earth. Green plants use sunlight to manufacture, or produce, food in a complex process called photosynthesis. In a healthy forest ecosystem, the food energy that plants manufacture travels, eventually, from plants to animals of all kinds, flesh-eaters as well as plant-eaters. Plants are the forest **producers**.

A seed cone, for example, develops as a tree grows from the energy it produces with the sun's assistance. The cone matures and drops into the forest's litter where it is eaten by a mouse. The mouse, by eating the plant material, unlocks for itself some of the food energy stored in the cone. At this point, the energy has moved one link along a

Opposite *Food energy that began with green plants travels another link when a great horned owl devours a mouse.*

chain. It has moved from producer to consumer. Later, the mouse is killed and eaten by a great horned owl, another consumer. Some of the energy originally stored in the seed cone has moved another link, this time to the owl.

Eventually the owl will die. Forest **decomposers**, those creatures that live on dead material, will eat the owl. In that way the energy first stored in the cone will move yet another link. More important, the activity of the decomposers—microscopic bacteria, earthworms, mites, fungi, and others—will cause the chemical breakdown of the owl. That process of reducing the owl's tissues to basic elements—nitrogen, carbon, iron, hydrogen, and more—will allow the elements to filter into the air and soil. There they will again be used by plants, and the energy will continue to flow from one organism in the forest to another.

The flow of energy is not always as compact as the link between owl and mouse. The interactions between plants, herbivores, and carnivores are often complex and involve several interlinking energy chains often called a **food web**.

In the forest it is apparent that the rate of energy flow is not steady. The season of the year has a major impact on the amount of activity in the forest communities.

Spring and summer are busy times, but the shortening days of autumn are a signal to slow the pace of activity. Nowhere is the change in pace more dramatic than in the deciduous forest, where the trees' autumn colors herald an end to the growing season.

Trees need water to function, but water is unavailable in the winter because the ground is frozen. To preserve the moisture already in their systems, trees shut down; they become **dormant**. Broad leaves, which allow a significant loss of moisture, are dropped.

The leaves are shed after the production of chlorophyll stops. Green chlorophyll, the substance that colors spring and summer leaves, is used by plants in the photosynthesis process. Since the tree is closing shop for the winter, it has no need for chlorophyll. When the remaining chlorophyll in a leaf fades away in September or October, the leaf reveals the color pigments that were already in the leaf and adds new ones.

As autumn advances, the separation layer of cells between leaf stem and branch forms. With each gust of wind and stinging rain, millions of leaves pinwheel to the forest bottom. As many as 10 million leaves may tumble down on one acre of woodland.

While the leaves fall, the energy level of the animal community is slackening too. Deer develop warm coats so that they can remain active in winter, but squirrels retreat to hollows and stick nests on the coldest days. The woodchuck and marmot *hibernate* in dens. Their body temperature drops almost to freezing. Their heartbeat slows, and these animals nap the winter away. Chipmunks and bears don't hibernate. Rather, they become **torpid**, or drowsy, a condition that requires the use of far less food and energy than they needed in the summer.

The bird population in the North American forests declines each fall, especially in the north. Most birds cannot find adequate food in the winter forest. The majority **migrate** to the southern states, Mexico, Central America, and South America.

CONSERVATION OF THE FOREST

A large portion of the boreal forest and many of our mountain forests have never been cut. They remain virgin woodland, and many of the tracts are forever protected in national, state, and provincial parks. The conifer region escaped the ax largely because its climate and terrain were not desirable for massive human settlement. There were exceptions, particularly in the Great Lakes area. Many of the forests in that region are "second growth," which means that a second forest has grown on the site of the original forest.

The deciduous, eastern forest did not fare as well because it became the residence of most of the American population and its early farming. By the 1850s much of New England, for example, had been deforested. Connecticut and Vermont, both of which were originally 75 percent forest, had been reduced to 25 percent forest. Now, however, both states have about 75 percent forest again, and two other New England states—New Hampshire and Maine—are about 85 percent forested.

Much of the forested land in the United States and Canada is owned by the government. Timber companies and land development companies also own substantial forest acreage.

Some of the forest in government ownership is completely protected from destruction. The national parks, and wilderness areas within the national forest system of the United States, are protected. Other tracts in the national forests are leased to timber companies for cutting. These areas are usually reseeded so that a new forest will grow.

Unlike Europe, which destroyed most of its original forest hundreds of years ago, North America retains a magnificent forest landscape. Some of the credit for that situation belongs to people like John Muir, who brought to the public's attention the beauty of western forests and the need to protect them.

The security of North America's forests should never be taken for granted, however. Arguments often arise about how to best use forest lands. Which government forest tracts should be leased for cutting, how should they be cut, and how should timbered areas be reseeded?

Some forests are more impressive

Opposite **Opposite** *Early morning shafts of sunlight bathe redwoods in Redwoods National Park, California.*

than others. Some have particularly out-standing **aesthetic** or **biological** value. People who are responsible for deciding which forests will be cut do not always agree, however, that a particular forest should be saved.

The method by which a forest is cut causes controversy because forests can be "clear cut" or "selectively cut." Clear cutting removes all the trees in a plot and sometimes encourages erosion. Selective cutting leaves some trees, but it reduces the timber yield and requires greater care, time, and effort on the part of the lumber company. Still, selective cutting is often important for the welfare of certain animals and for the stability of the soil. Leaving some trees is often necessary to prevent mudslides from damaging streams and rivers.

The reseeding of a cut forest often involves replanting the ground with fast-growing pines. The original forest may have been a mixture of tree species, even a hardwood forest. Forests of mixed species and sizes are much more useful to wildlife than a uniform forest of pines.

Problems with **exotics**, non-native species, also beset forests. The American chestnut has been virtually wiped out by the chestnut blight, a disease unintentionally imported on lumber around 1900. Dutch elm disease has destroyed thousands of American elms. Gypsy moths, released in 1869 after importation to the United States, period-ically **defoliate** thousands of acres of eastern forest. In Florida, the Australian "pine" and eucalyptus and the Brazilian pepper tree are invading and destroying forests of native trees.

In California, the massive red-woods that grow outside the state parks and Redwoods National Park remain embattled and vulnerable to logging. In Alaska, environmentalists and the National Forest Service quarrel over the fate of mossy rain forests in the Tongass National Forest. Likewise, the lumber industry and environmentalists also often disagree. Ultimately, these con-flicting viewpoints will probably lead to the total protection of some key forests and to the lumbering of others.

Meanwhile, the forests remain one of the continent's greatest natural attrac-tions and resources. They are a haven for wildlife and people alike.

GLOSSARY

adaptation   a characteristic of function, form, or behavior that improves an organism's survival chances in a particular habitat

aesthetic   relating to the beauty of something

aquatic   of or referring to water

arboreal   tree-dwelling

biological   relating to a living thing

camouflage   an organism's ability to blend in with its surroundings

carnivore   meat-eating animal

coniferous   relating to a conifer, a plant that bears seeds in cones, especially needle-leaved trees

deciduous   plant that periodically loses its leaves, typically broad-leaved trees in the autumn

decomposer   an organism, most often bacteria and fungi, that consumes dead tissue and reduces it to small particles

defoliate   to remove the leaves or foliage from a plant

dormant   a state of inactivity due to the slowing or stopping of normal functions

ecosystem   a system of exchanges of food and energy between plants and animals and their environment

exotic   a plant or animal introduced into an environment in which it does not naturally occur

food web   the network of interlocking food chains

habitat   an animal's or plant's immediate surroundings; its specific place within the community

herb   a flowering plant with a soft rather than woody stem

herbivore   plant-eating animal

invertebrate   an animal without a backbone

migrate   to make a predictable and seasonal movement from one location to another some distance away

omnivore   an animal with the capability to eat both plant and animal material

photosynthesis   the process by which green plants produce simple food sugars through the use of sunlight and chlorophyll

pioneer plants   plants that are the first to grow in a newly-available habitat

producer   a green plant, so named for its ability to manufacture, or produce, food

resinous   a particular type of plant secretion

succession   the gradual replacement of one plant community by another

temperate   referring to that part of the earth in the Northern Hemisphere between the tropic of Cancer at 23½° north of the equator and the Arctic Circle at 66° north of the equator

torpid   a condition of deep sleep

vetebrate   a animal with a backbone

FOREST SITES

The following is a sampling of outstanding sites where you can expect to find characteristic plants and animals of the forest and outstanding forest scenery:

CANADA

Alberta
Banff National Park, Banff, Alberta
Jasper National Park, Jasper, Alberta
British Columbia
Pacific Rim National Park, Ucluelet, British Columbia
Nova Scotia
Kejimkujik National Park, Maitland Bridge, Nova Scotia
Ontario
Pukaskwa National Park, Marathon, Ontario

UNITED STATES

Alaska
Tongass National Forest, Juneau, Alaska
Arizona
Coconino National Forest, Flagstaff, Arizona
California
Redwoods National Park, Crescent City, California
Sequoia National Park, Three Rivers, California
Colorado
Rocky Mountain National Park, Estes Park, Colorado
Florida
Apalachicola National Forest, Tallahassee, Florida
Ocala National Forest, Ocala, Florida
Georgia
Chattahoochee National Forest, Gainesville, Georgia
Maine
Baxter State Park, Millinocket, Maine
Montana
Glacier National Park, West Glacier, Montana
New Hampshire
White Mountains National Forest, Laconia, New Hampshire
New York
Adirondack State Park, Albany, New York
North Carolina
Great Smoky Mountains National Park, Gatlinburg, Tennessee
Pisgah National Forest, Asheville, North Carolina
Oregon
Willamette National Forest, Eugene, Oregon
Washington
Mount Baker-Snoqualmie National Forest, Seattle, Washington
West Virginia
Monongahela National Forest, Elkins, West Virginia

ACTIVITIES

Here are some activities and projects that will help you learn more about the North American forests:

1. Choose one of the forest animals and find out how it is specifically made (adapted) for life in the forest environment.

2. Design a travel brochure for a particular forested region. Describe the area's plants, animals, and scenic value. Tell what clothes would be appropriate and why. Tell how to reach the area and how someone would get around once there. Why would people want to go there? What would they be able to do there?

3. Draw a food chain or several food chains, showing the relationship of sunlight to plants, plants to animals, and animals to each other in a forest environment.

4. Report on one of the major forest preserves in the United States or Canada (see list in this book for ideas). Write to the appropriate site for information.

5. Build a diorama in a cardboard box. Paint a forest background and use cardboard, clay, or plaster of Paris figures of representative forest plants, animals, and features.

6. If you live near a forest, create a guide to the trees of your area by making a collection of leaves or leaf rubbings. One way to preserve leaves is to lay each leaf between several sheets of newspaper. Put books on top of the newspaper sheets to compress the leaf. After a week, the leaf should be dry and ready for attachment by tape or glue to cardboard or a scrapbook page. Make a leaf rubbing by first putting the leaf on a hard, flat surface, making sure to keep the veins up. Place a piece of paper over the leaf. Remove the wrapper from a crayon and rub the side of the crayon over the paper on top of the leaf.

7. Join a conservation organization that promotes the protection of forest plants, animals, and wilderness. Several national and international organizations are listed here:

UNITED STATES

Defenders of Wildlife
1244 Nineteenth St., NW
Washington, DC 20036

National Audubon Society
Membership Data Center
P.O. Box 2666
Boulder, CO 80322

National Wildlife Federation
1412 Sixteenth St., NW
Washington, DC 20036

The Nature Conservancy
1800 N. Kent St.
Arlington, VA 22209

The Sierra Club
730 Polk St.
San Francisco, CA 94109

CANADA

Canadian Nature Federation
75 Albert St., Suite 203
Ottawa, Ontario K1P 9Z9

National and Provincial
   Parks Assn. of Canada
Suite 308, 47 Colborne St.
Toronto, Ontario M5E 9Z9

The Young Naturalist Foundation
59 Front St. E.
Toronto, Ontario M5E 1B3

INDEX

Numbers in boldface type refer to photo pages.

47